NEW ENGLAND FALL FOLIAGE

PHOTOGRAPHS BY ELIZABETH KRAMER

THIS IS PART OF THE **VISITING** SERIES.

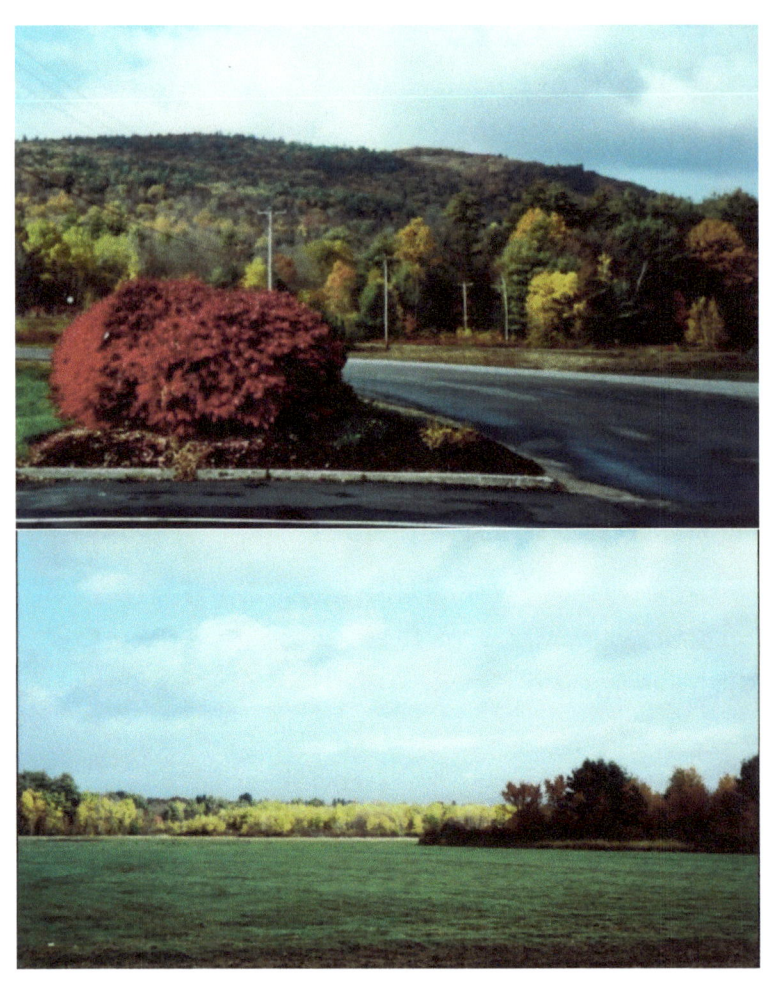

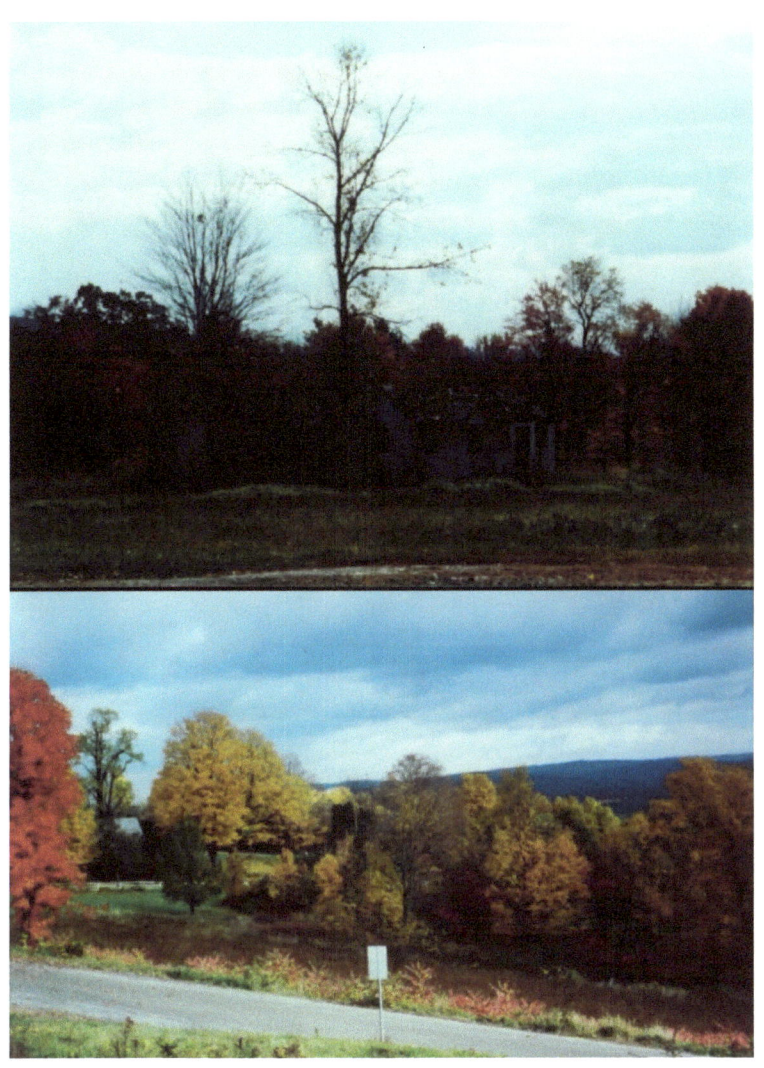

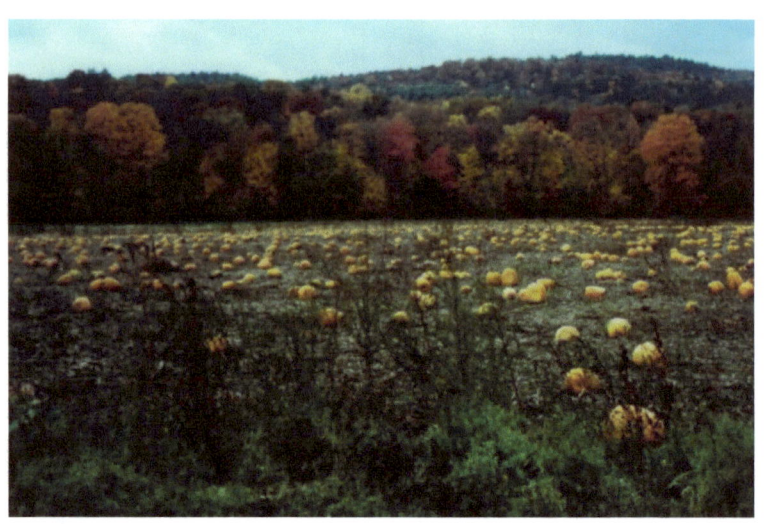

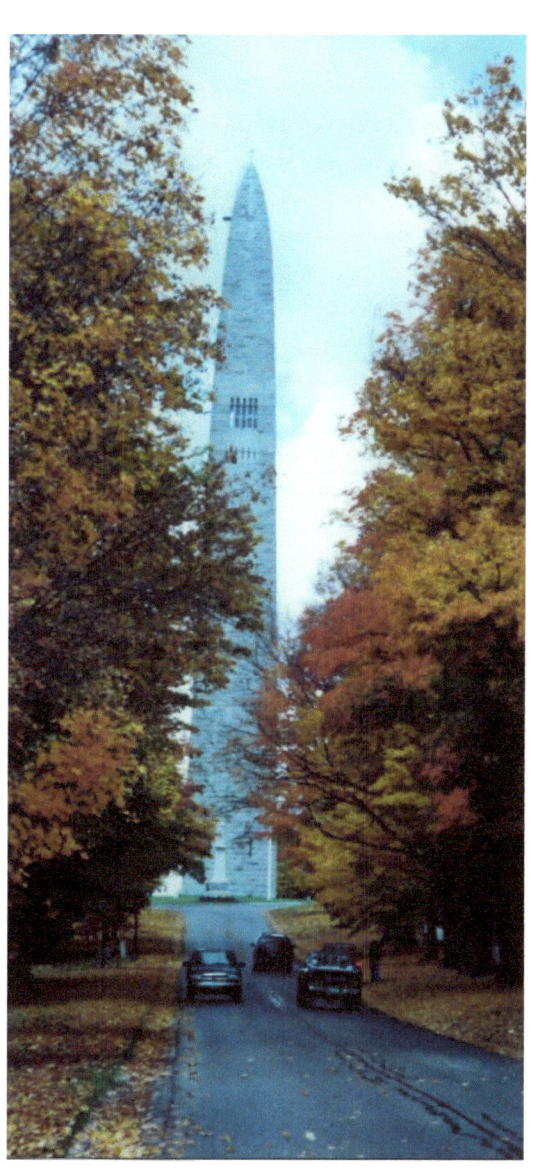

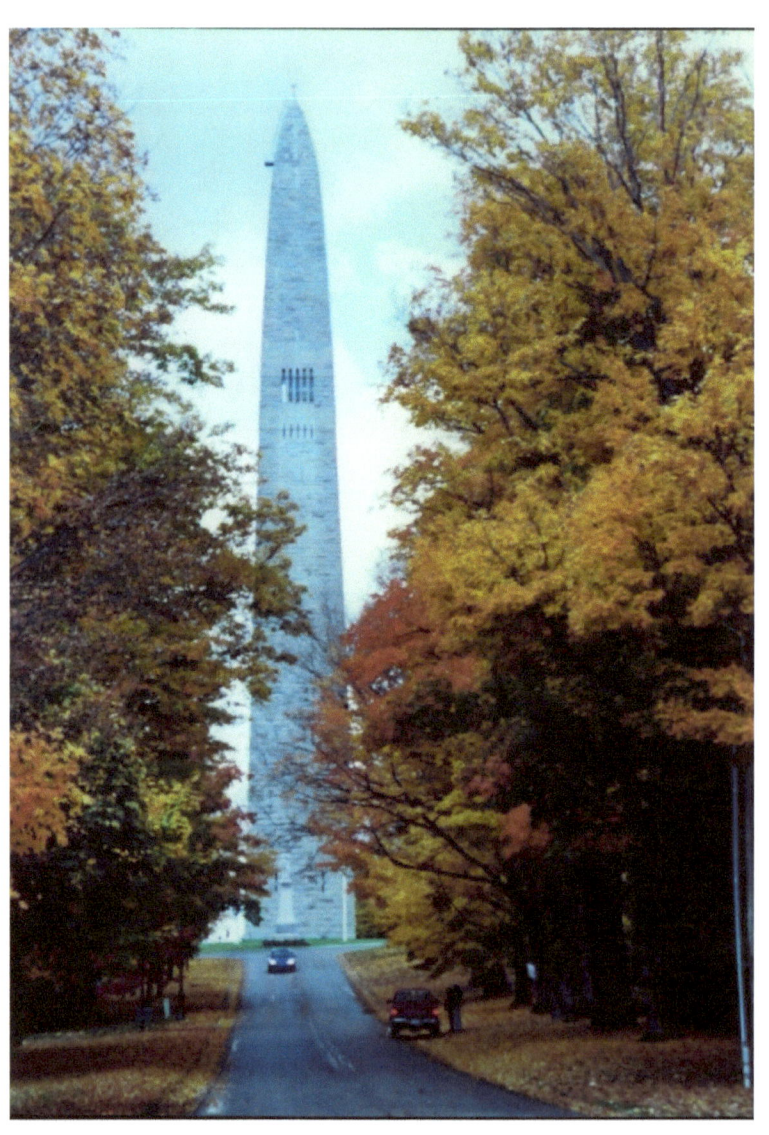

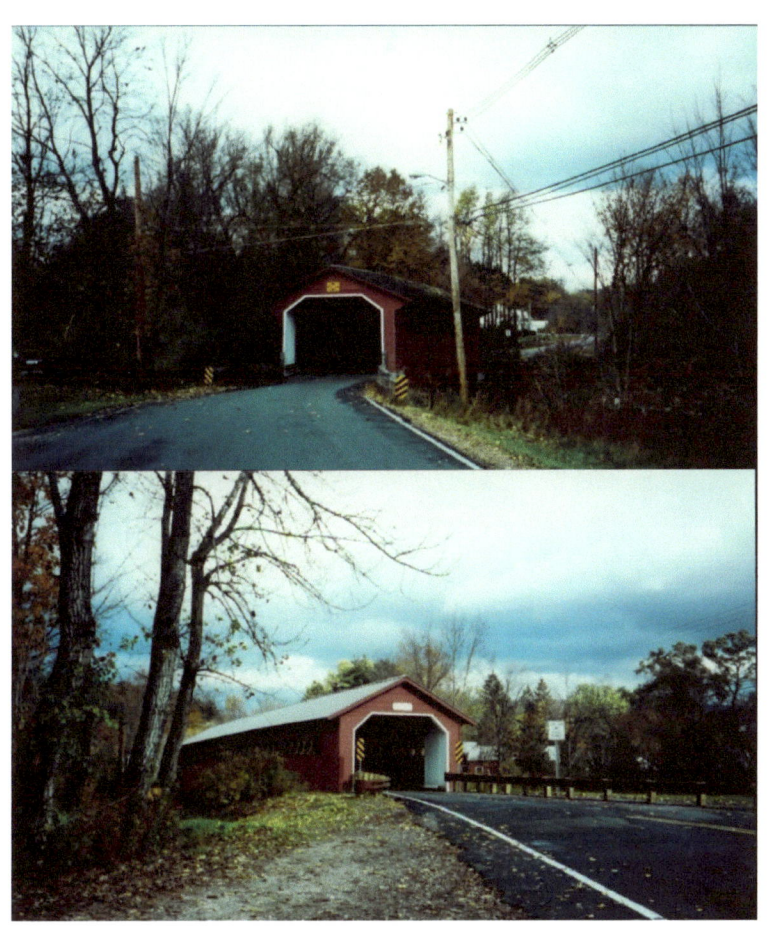

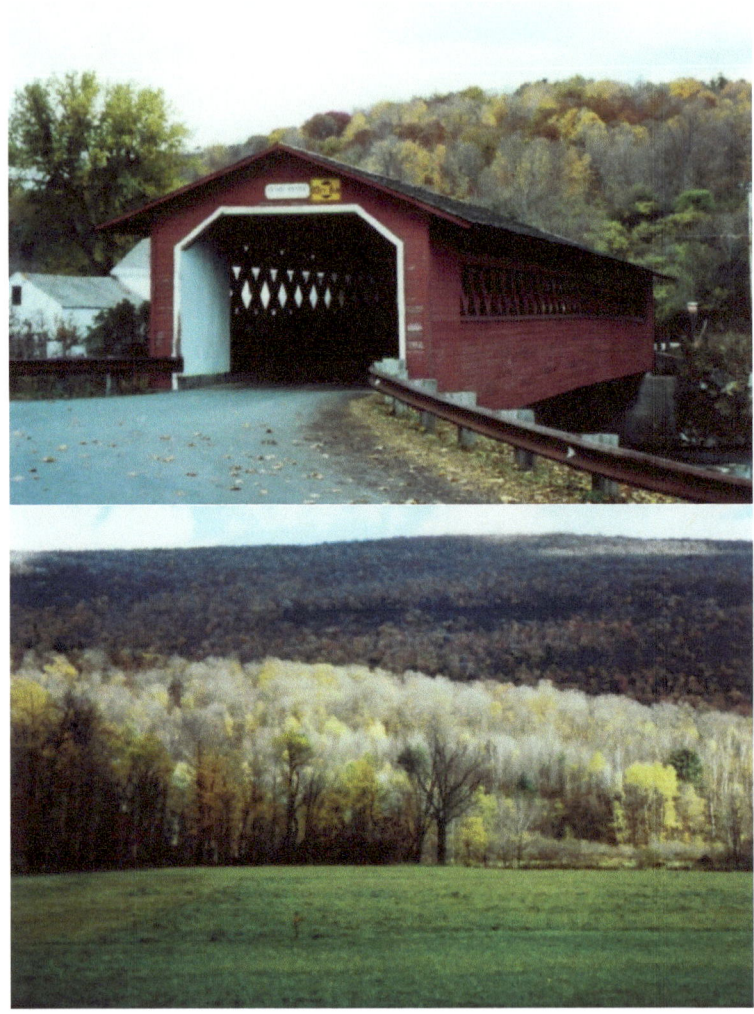

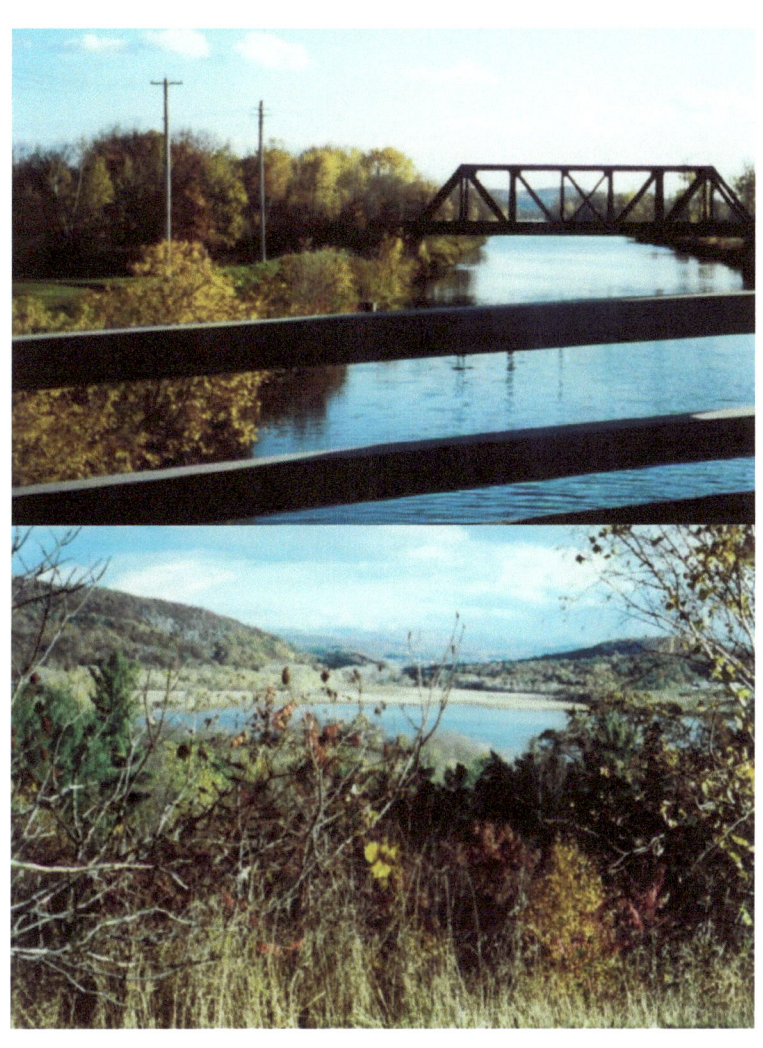

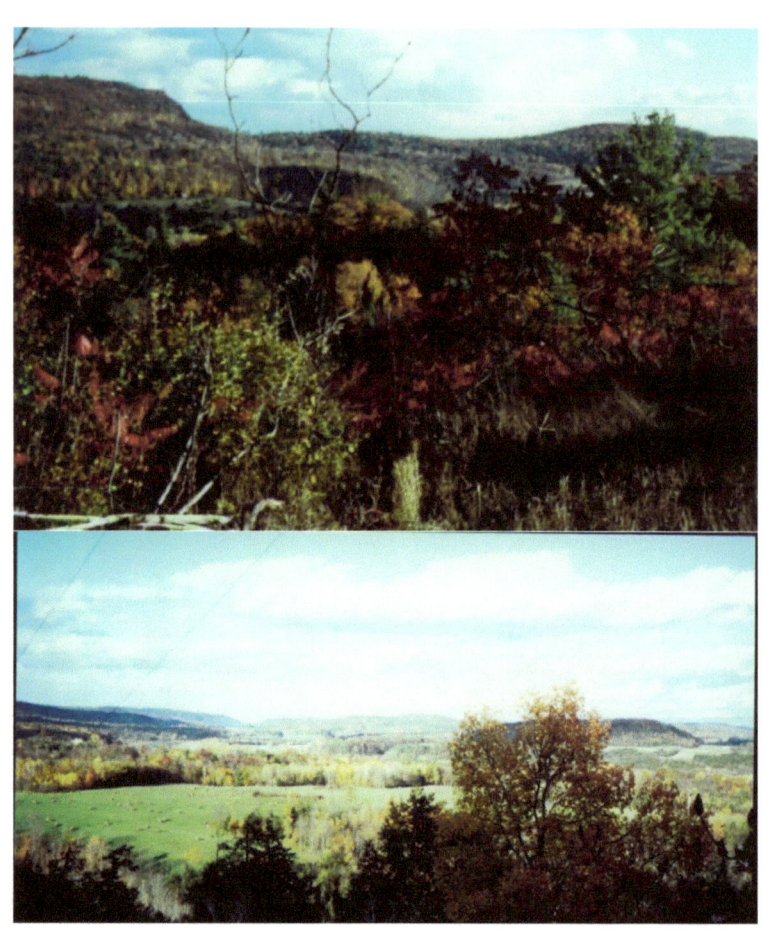

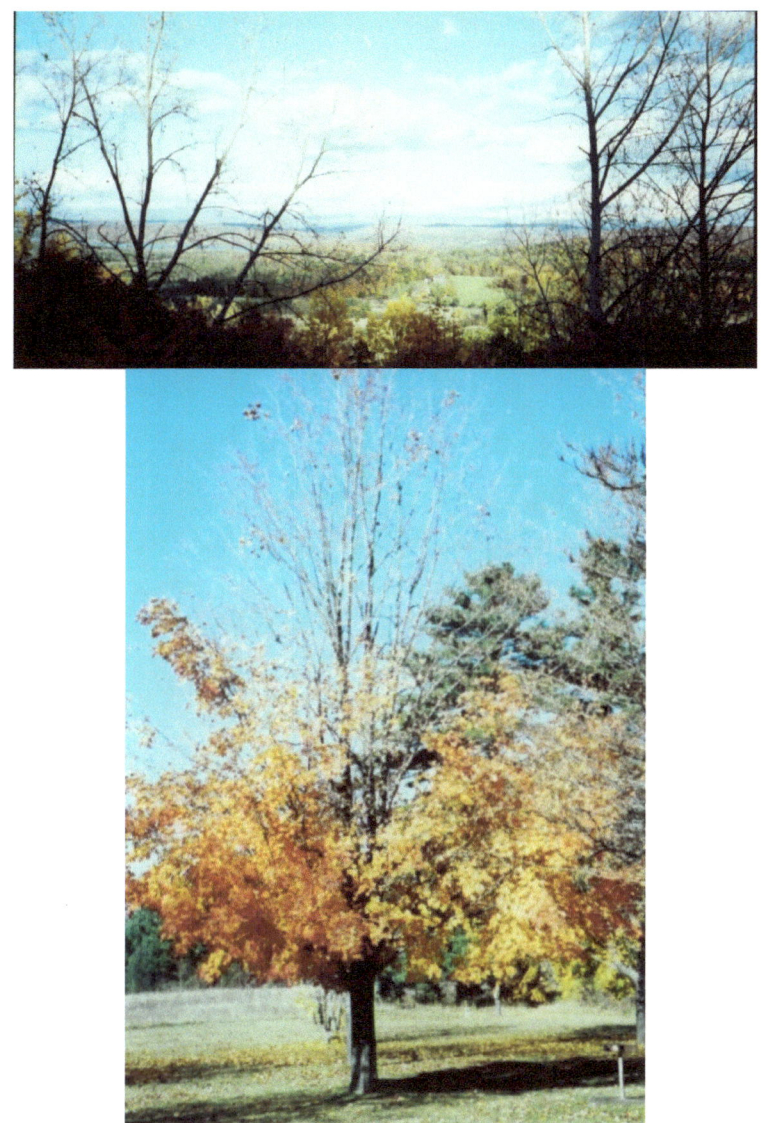

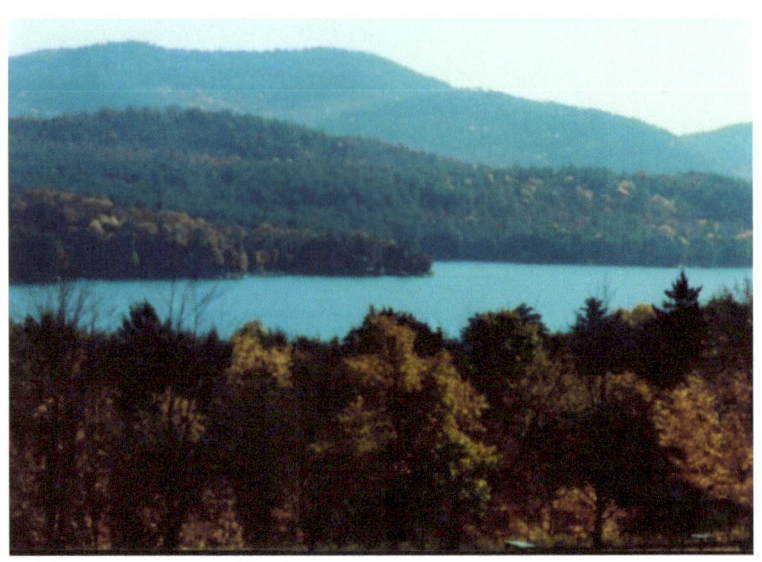

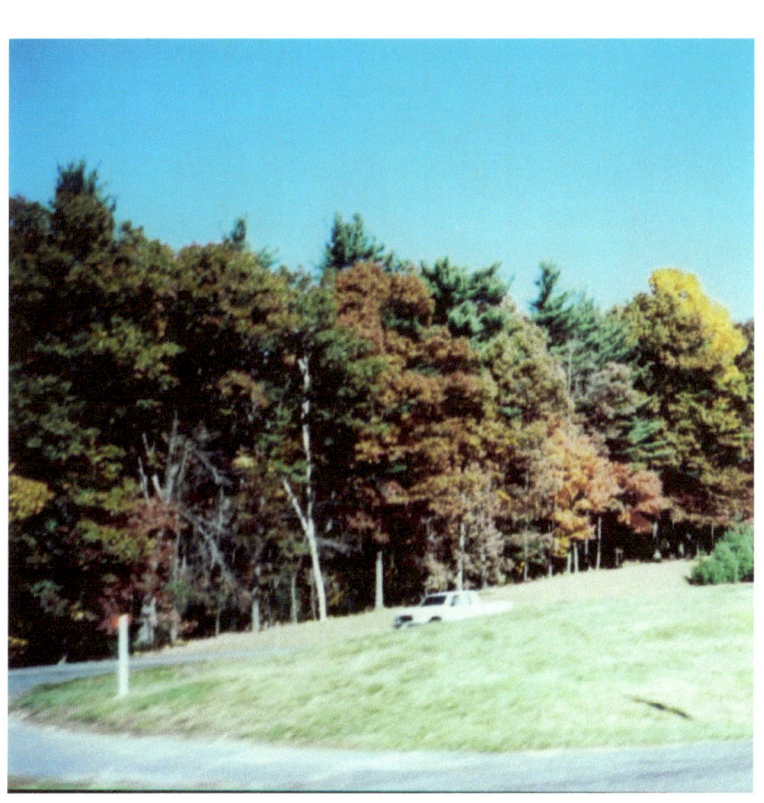

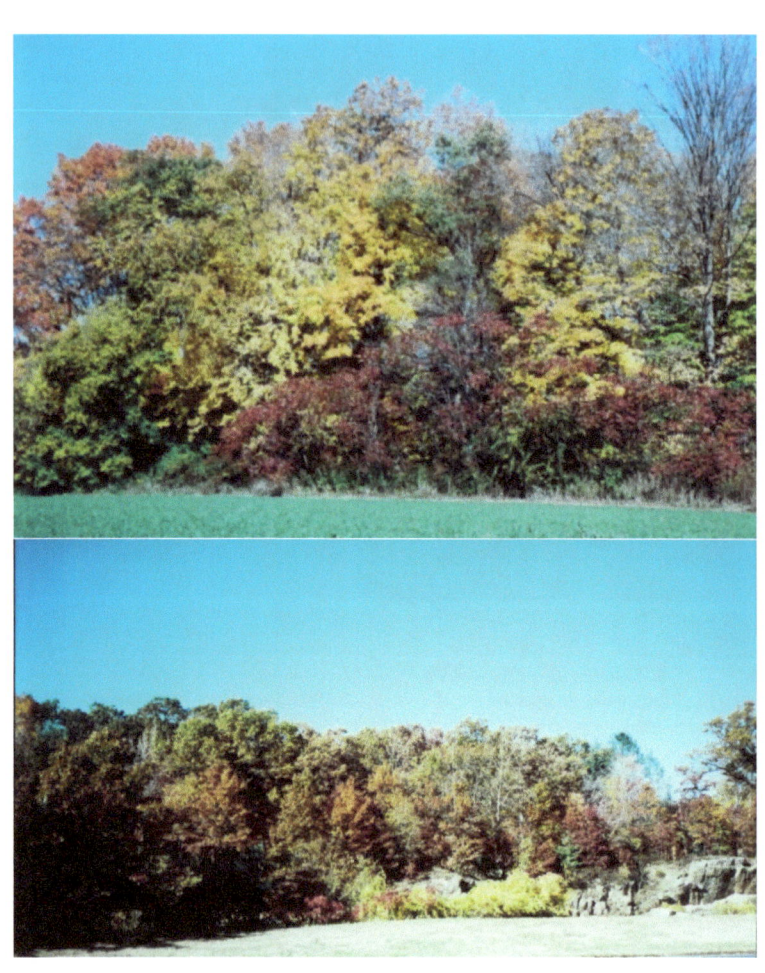

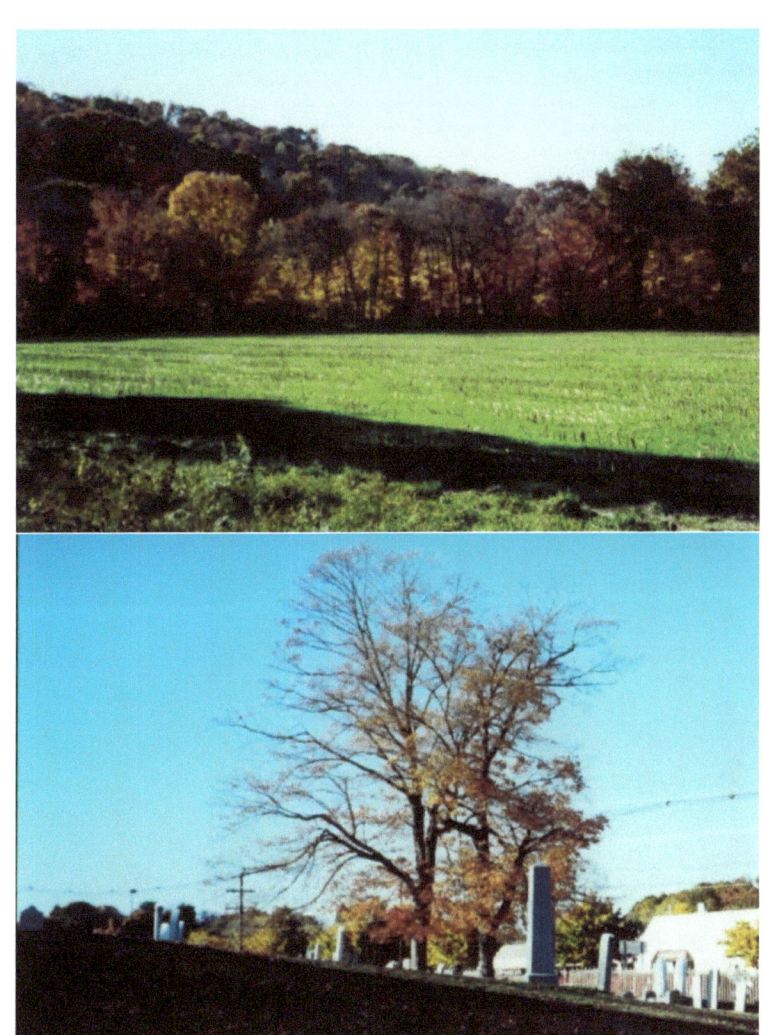

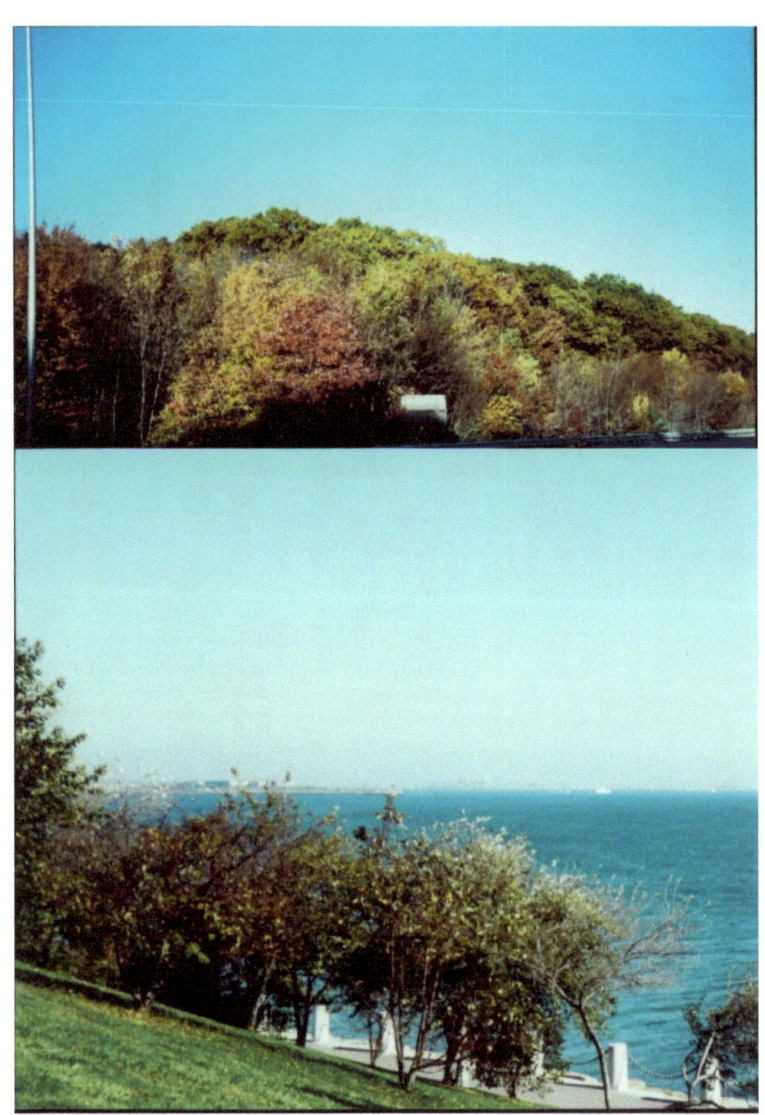

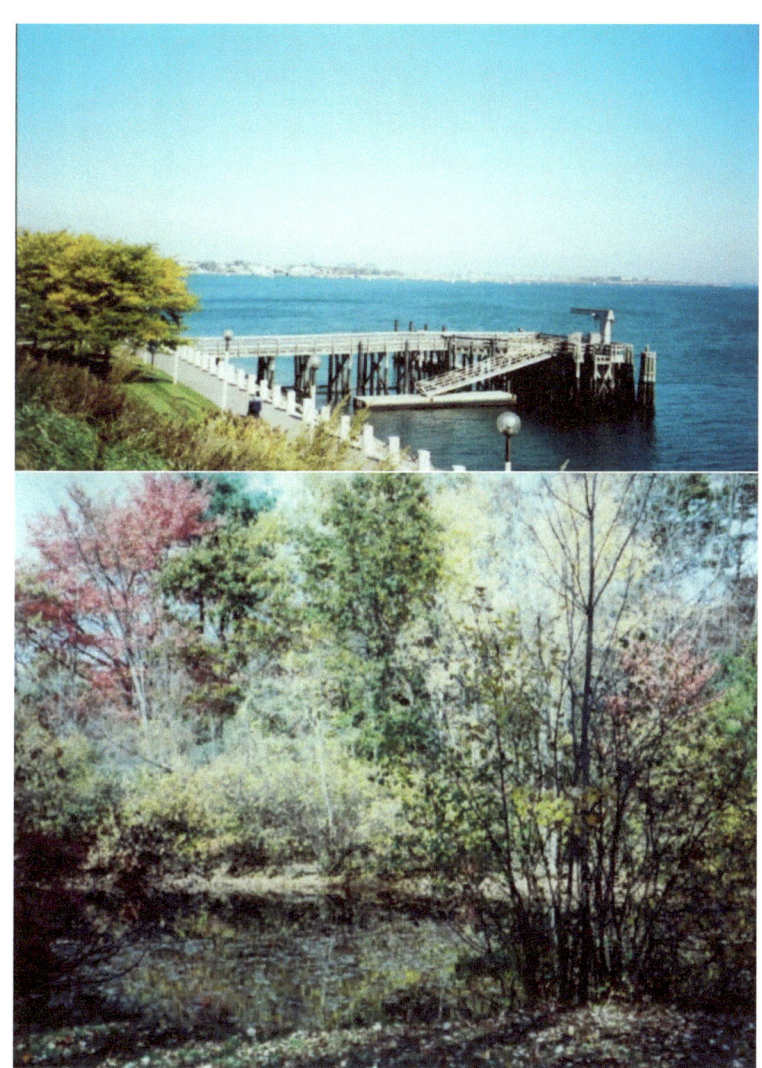

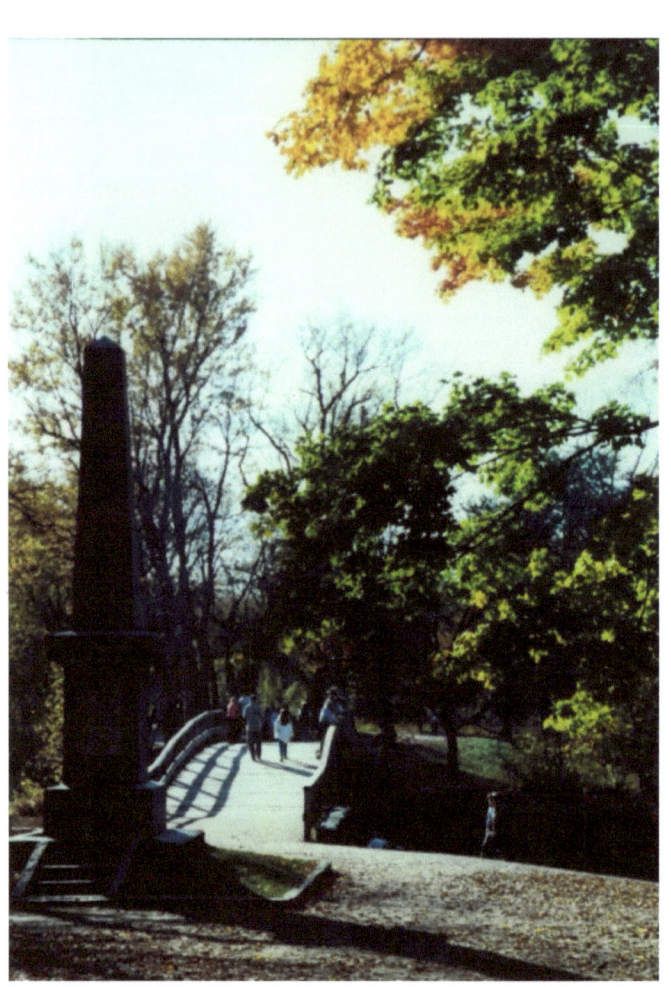

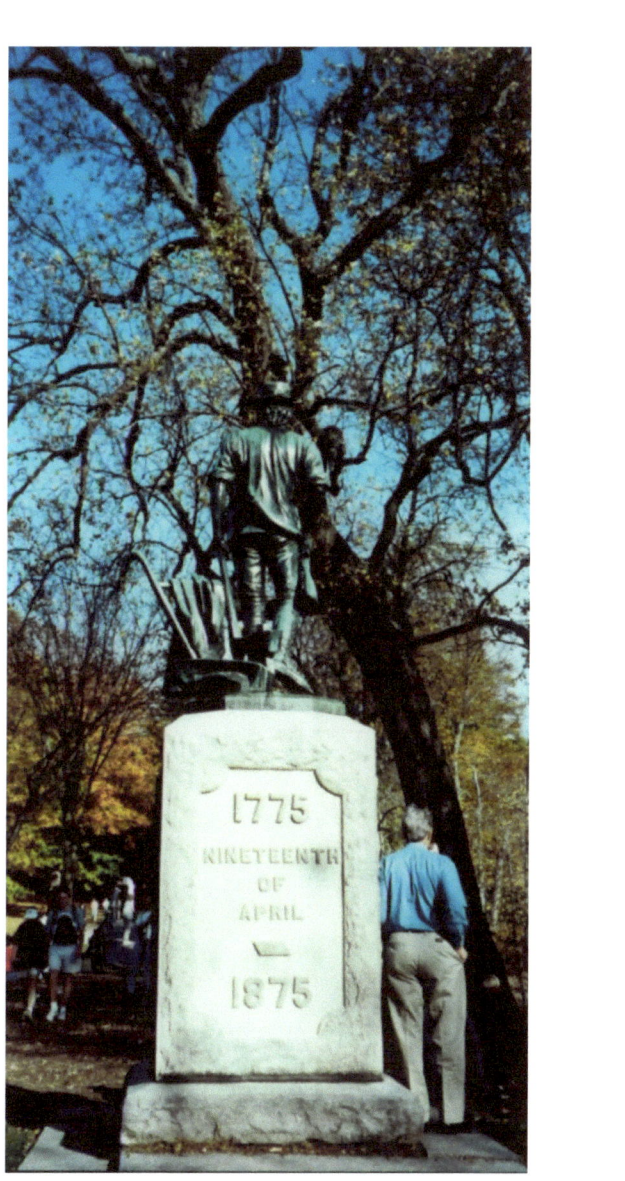

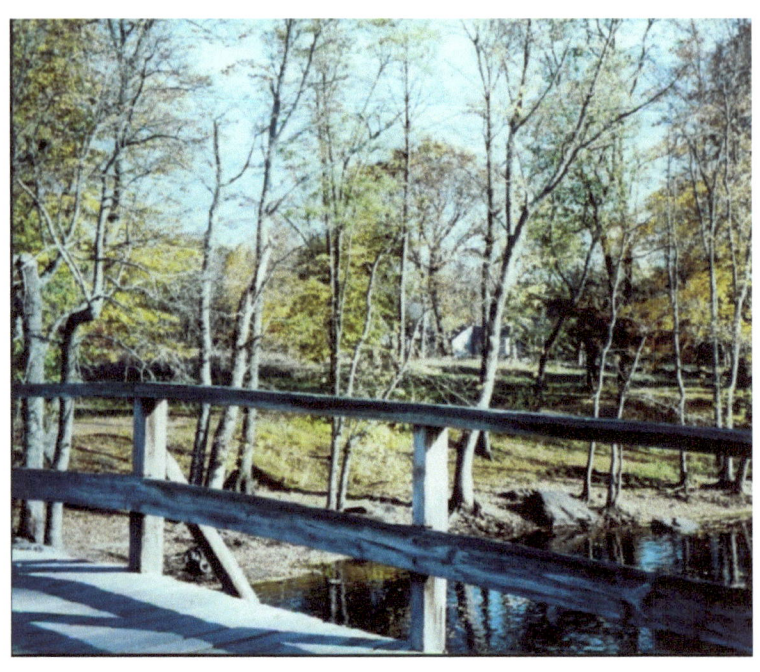

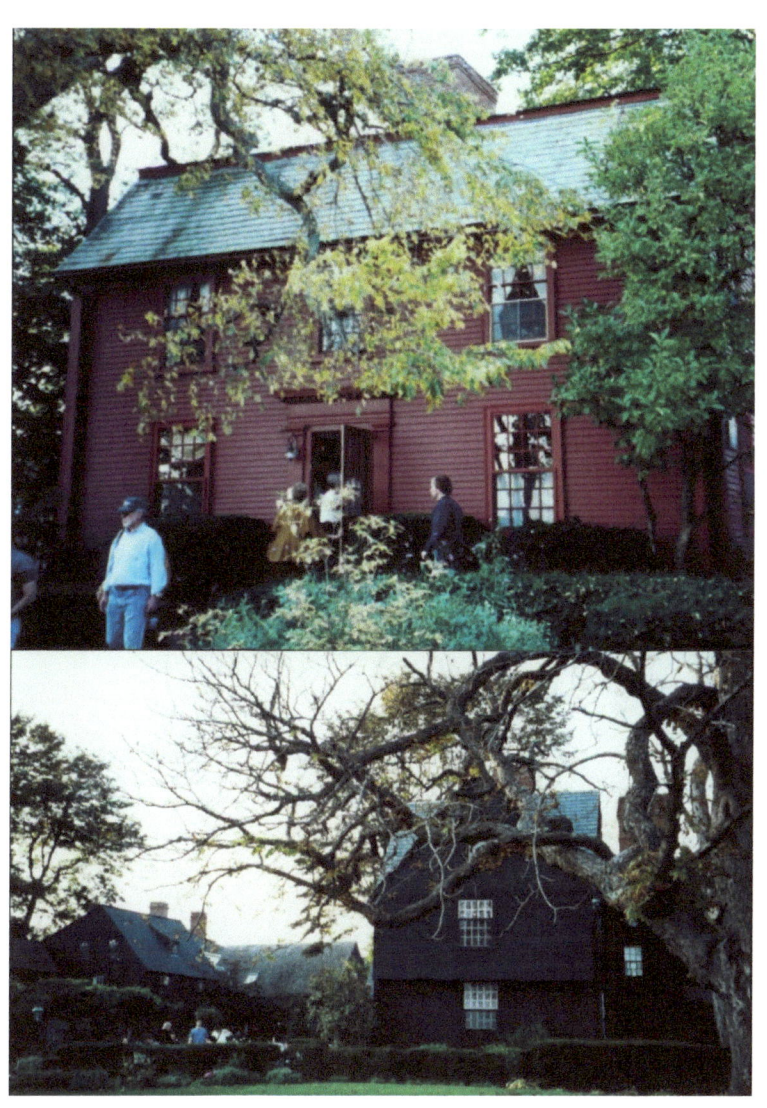

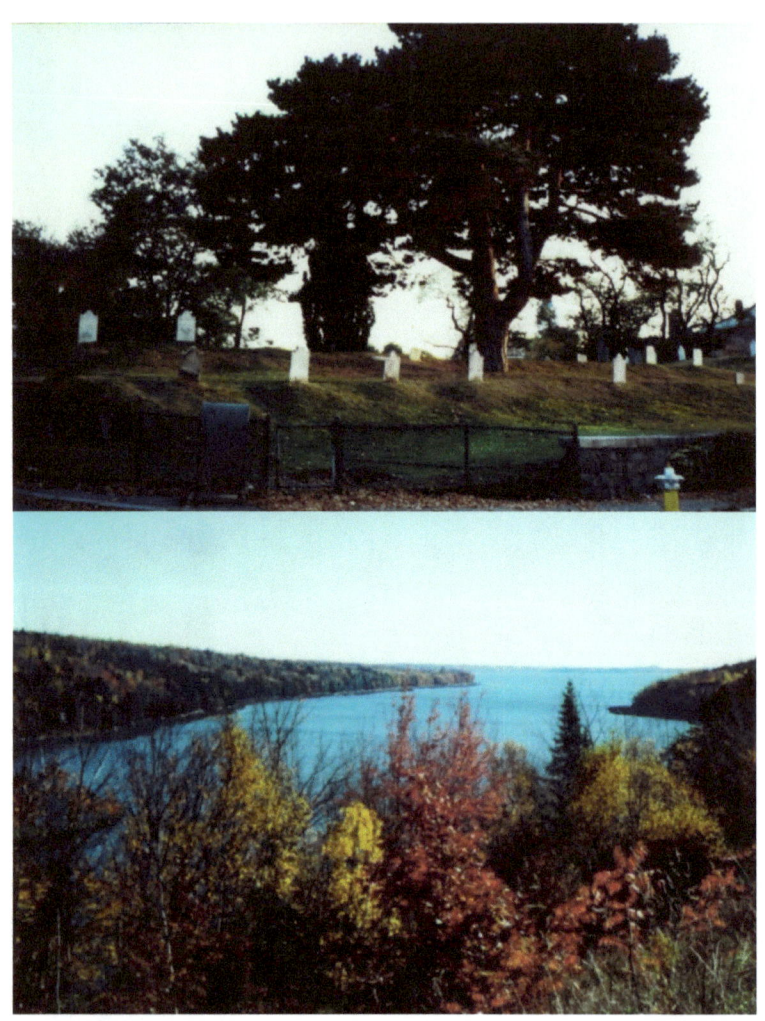

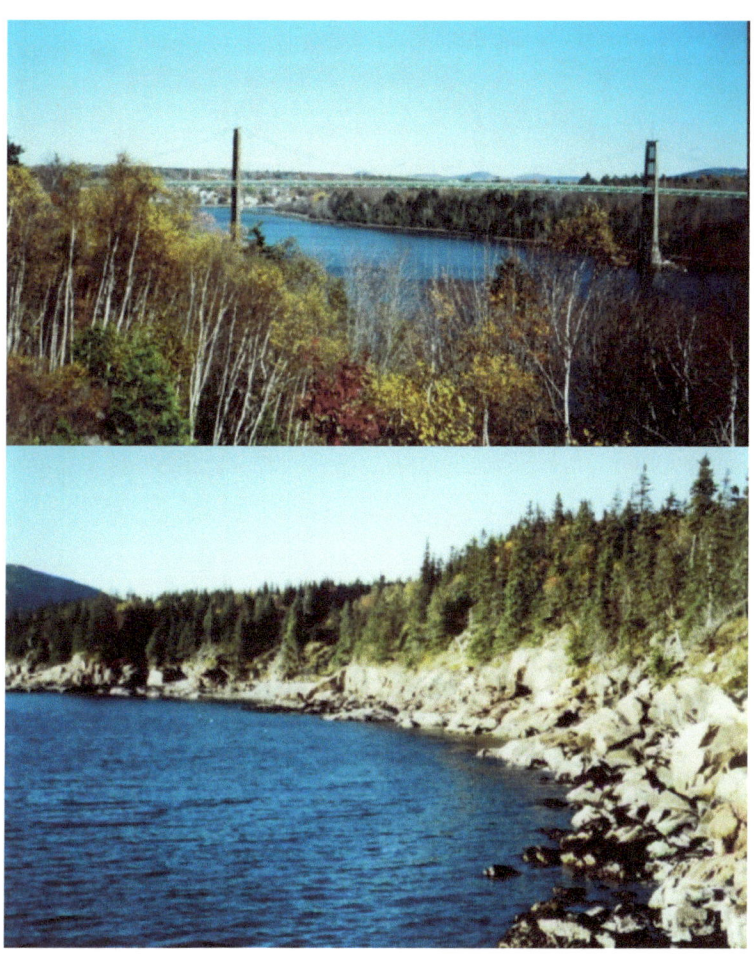

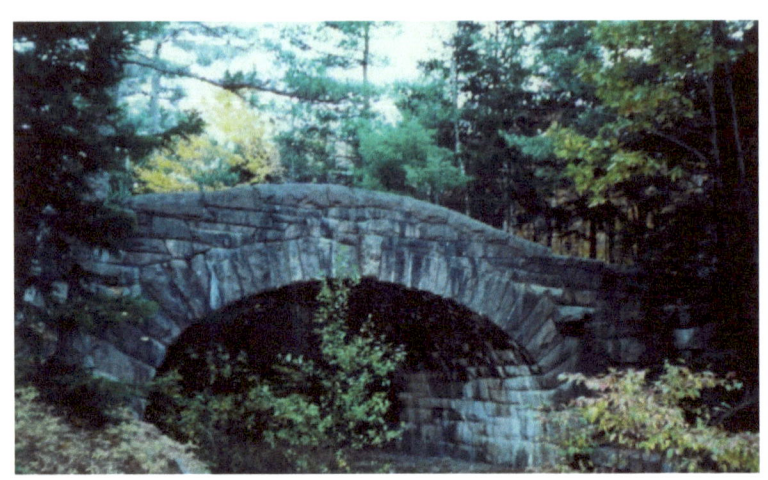

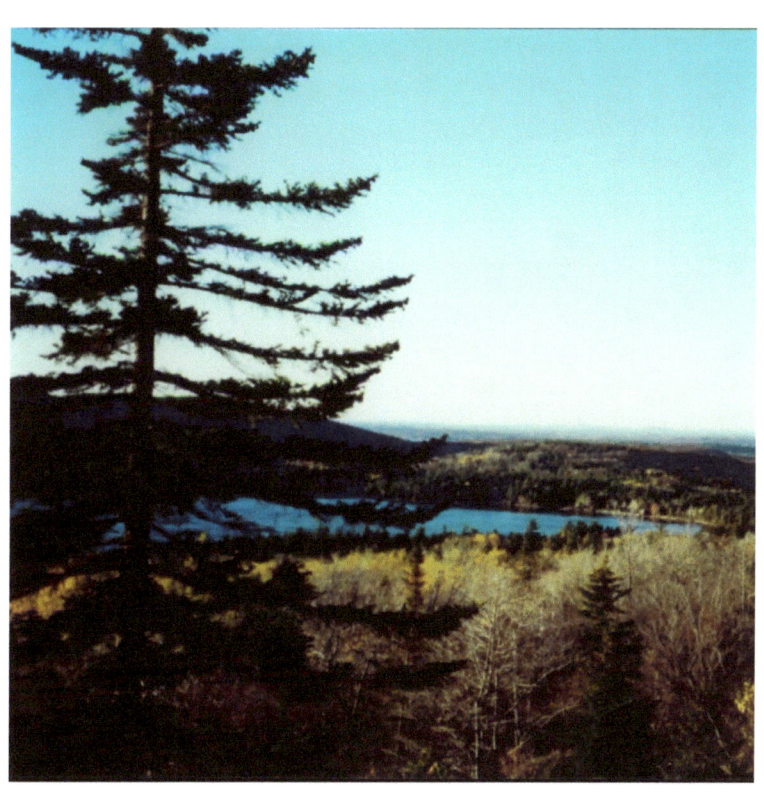

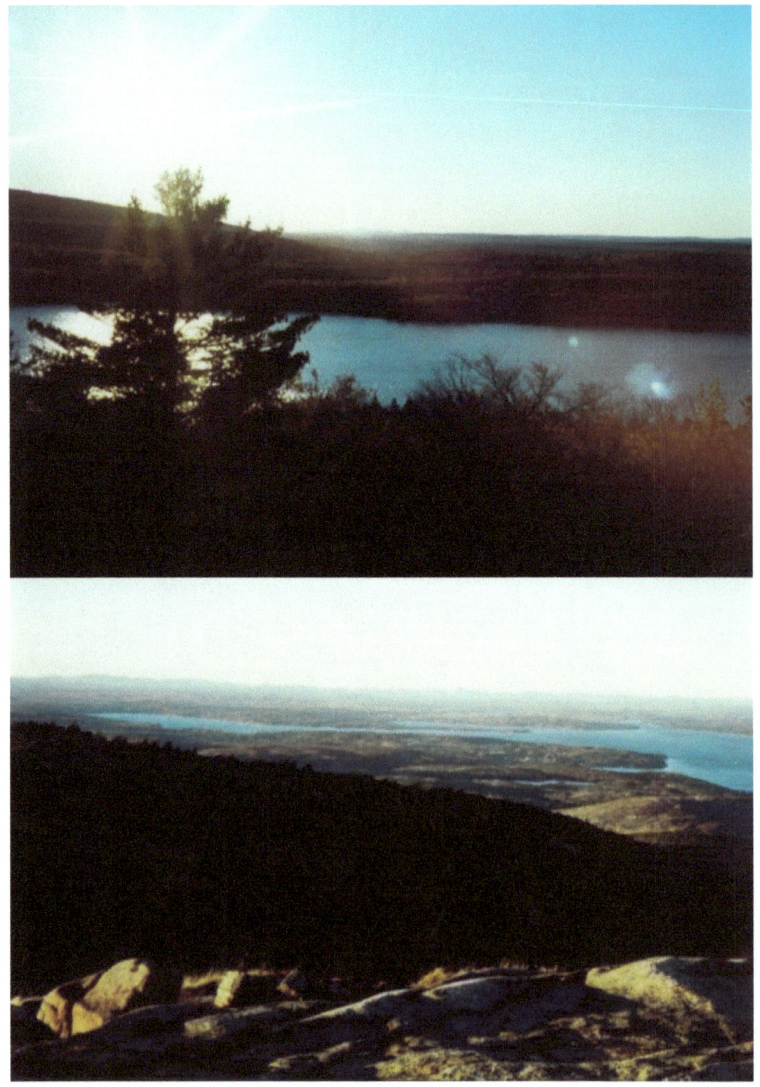

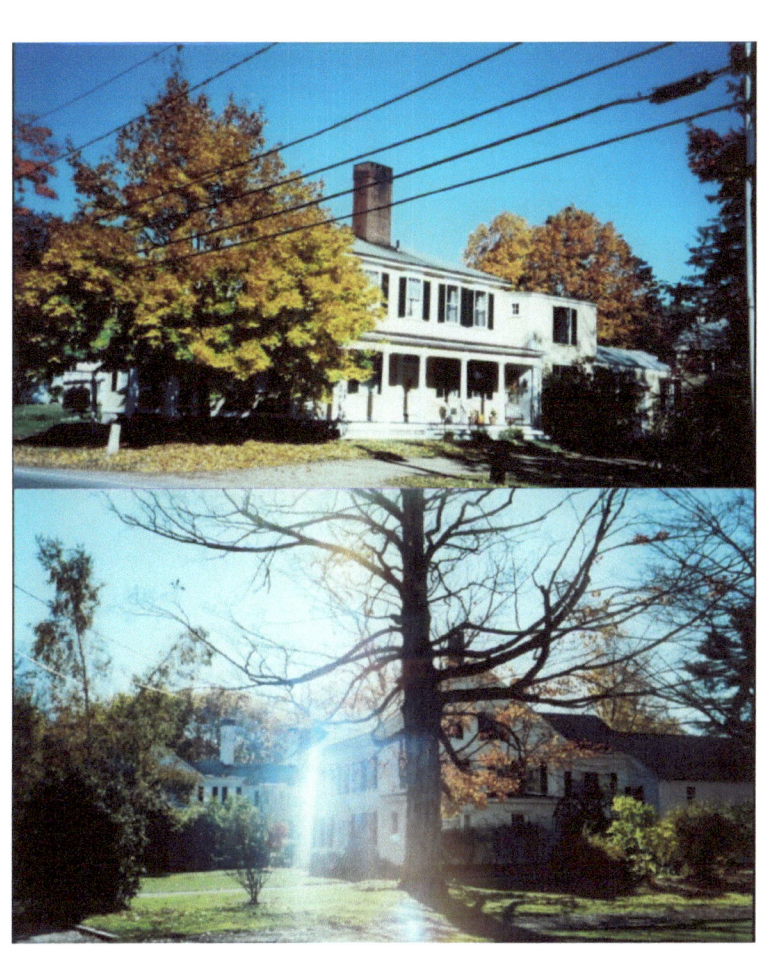

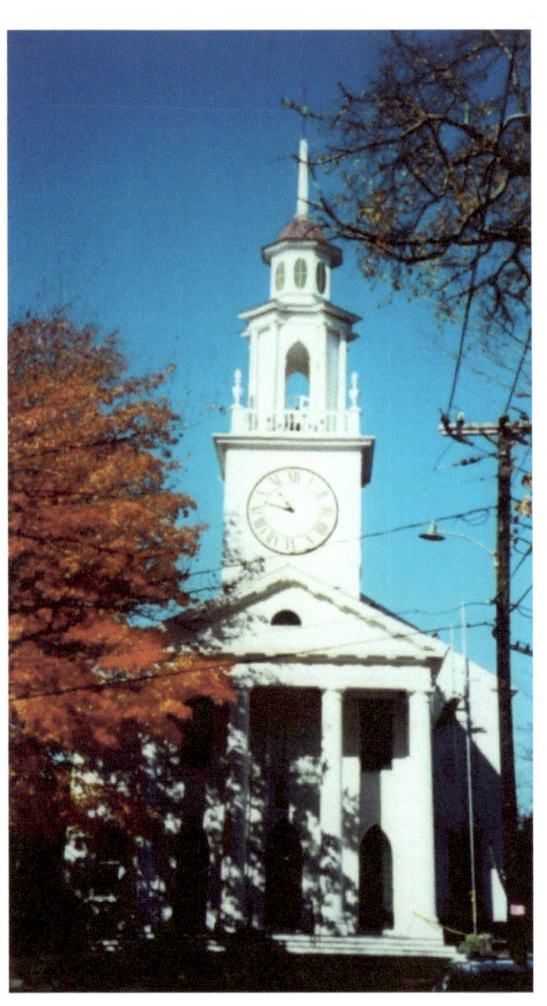

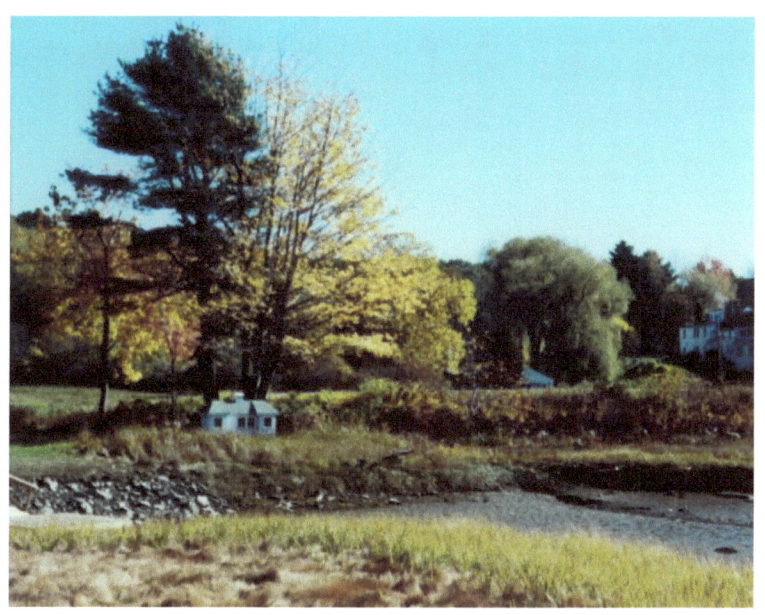

www.ingramcontent.com/pod-product-compliance
Lightning Source LLC
Chambersburg PA
CBHW041616180526
45159CB00002BC/877